Dinosaur Stomp!

By Crystal Bowman
and Nancy Faber
Illustrated by Joel E. S. Tanis

Dinosaur Stomp!

FJH BOOKS and DOVETREE BOOKS
2525 Davie Road, Suite 360
Fort Lauderdale, FL 33317-7424

FJH BOOKS is a part of THE FJH MUSIC COMPANY INC.

ISBN 1-56939-277-3 FB1000

Printed and bound in U.S.A.

10 9 8 7 6 5 4 3 2 1

Art Direction by Gwen Terpstra.
The text of this book is set in Sand.
The illustrations are rendered in watercolor and colored pencil.
Typography by Gwen Terpstra.

To Beth, our new addition to the family. ***Chris***

To William Nesbitt, who at three could make great dinosaur sounds on the piano. ***Nancy***

For Kathy. Special thanks to Avery, Dad, and Schoon vacations. ***Joel***

Songs about lions and
bears are inviting.

Songs about tigers are
always exciting.

Alligator songs are
snappy and fun.

But the Dinosaur Stomp
is my favorite one.

Oh my!

CRASH!

BOOM!

RUMBLE!

THUMP!

My fingers make
the low keys jump.

This music makes me
roar and romp.

I love to play the
Dinosaur Stomp!

But as I play
the very last note,

My piano spins
and starts to float.

SWISH!

WHOOSH!

ZIM!

ZAM!

Like magic
I'm in dinosaur land!

CRASH!

THUNK!

RUMBLE!

BOOM!

They like my
prehistoric tune.

Big feet pounding,
mighty roars,

Make way- here come
the dinosaurs!

First I spy
an Apatosaurus

Stomping, romping
through the forest.

Smashing, crashing
down the trail

With his mighty
monster tail.

Stegosaurus
wants a snack.

Yikes! Big spikes
are on his back!

On the plants
he munches, crunches,

Eating leafy,
lazy lunches.

Tyrannosaurus Rex
is near.

How do I get
out of here?

Can you see his
pointed claws?

Do you hear
his grinding jaws?

Wow! It's fierce
Triceratops.

It's time to hide
when this beast stops.

Pointed horns –
one, two, three,

I'll just scoot
past quietly.

Diplodocus
has a monster foot.

Have you had a
close-up look?

Giant footprints
in the sand

As he rumbles
through the land.

Apotosaurus,
Stegosaurus,

Tyrannosaurus Rex.

Triceratops,
Diplodocus,

What comes next?

CRASH!

BOOM!

TAKE OFF!

FLY!

Pterodactyls
in the sky.

They sweep and sway
and screech about.

"Give my music back!"
I shout.

Then suddenly
there is no sound.

No dinosaurs
are stomping around.

No more footprints,
no more trees–

Just me and
my piano keys.

Should I play
the song once more?

We're sure to meet
a dinosaur!

JEST

Dinosaur Stomp

Nancy and Randall Faber
from *Piano Adventures®*

Slow and heavy

About Piano Adventures®

Piano Adventures® is an acclaimed piano method series by Nancy and Randall Faber. It has become the method of choice among leading music educators across North America. If you have taken piano lessons as a child, you will appreciate this exciting transformation in piano teaching. Piano Adventures® offers the combination of fun and challenge with its appealing repertoire, music theory applied to both popular and classical idioms, and special techniques for developing artistry.

About Piano Adventures® Storybooks

The Piano Adventures® Storybooks open with a little boy or girl sitting down to play a favorite piano piece. As the melody soars, the piano magically transports the child and the reader to an imaginary world where the fantastic can happen. Each story is based on a piece from the Piano Adventures® course, each with its own unique adventure. Whether you find yourself in the land of gigantic dinosaurs or in the miniature world of busy ants, you will delight in this celebration of musical creativity and childhood imagination.

Visit us at www.pianoadventures.com to learn how piano study can develop valuable life skills for your child.